Human Writes

Hasan Davis, J.D.

an imprint of Martin Sisters Publishing Company, Inc.

Published by JustUs Books,
an imprint of
Martin Sisters Publishing Company, Inc.
www. martinsisterspublishing.com
Copyright © 2019 Hasan Davis

Published in the United States
by Martin Sisters Publishing Company, Inc.

ISBN: 978-1-62553-100-1
Poetry
Advocacy

Edited by Merrill J. Davies
Printed in the United States of America

GRATITUDE

I arrived draped in anger.
A first attempt to explore this new world,
It almost killed me.

But there were those among you
Willing to stand at my side, and back,
To afford me other chances to fly.

From new heights, now
I show these wings, glistening in the sun.

Spread like the Phoenix--
Vibrant, reflecting every thought,
smile, and wish--
All of the dreams you held in place for me.

So now, my journey begins.
And like the Sankofa Bird
I glance back at those who have
Freed my wings of damaging debris
That I might move forward more gracefully,

With a silent tear of gratitude
With a strong, purposeful heart
I whisper graciously,

"Thank you."

DEDICATION

This collection is dedicated to my loving and supportive family (as I define it). Without them I could never have imagined wings this strong or reached summits this high.

To my parents Alice Lovelace and Charles "Jikki" Riley, thank you for inspiring me to always seek my greater self. To my wife Dreama and ons Malcolm and Christopher, thank you for anchoring me to my truth and giving me purpose.

To my siblings, by blood shared or sacrificed, Theresa, Tony, Shawnta, Sean and Derrick, thank you being uniquely amazing. Each of you showed me a greatness that I wanted to emulate in this world.

To the Affrilachian Poets who took me into their creative family and made me feel like I was home, a special thanks.

To Patty, thank you for providing us refuge from the world. To Dr. Lorraine Wilson, my champion, thank you for being courageous or foolish enough to carry fire in your open hands.

And finally, to Keith A. Goode, best friend, advisor, and godfather to my boys. A lifetime was too short a moment, but I am glad we had it, brother.

book one

book two

book three

when hope trumps fear

book one

skin deep

I never understood how something an eighth of a centimeter deep could leave such devastating craters in the landscape of our shared humanity.

BLACK ICARUS

(On meeting Lt. Col. A. Jefferson)

He,
Flying high into the sun on wings of pride,
Carried the weight of a people between broad black
shoulders.

Then,
Like sands through a broken hourglass,
Black Icarus fell back to earth
To walk again amongst those he guarded with courage
unbound.

In my ignorance,
I failed to recognize him for what he was.
This Knight, Sky Warrior, descended back to mortal grounds.

His vigil over,
Now he only flies in his dreams.

As a child I heard tales from grown folk
Who were not supposed to believe in myth.

But they did whisper his legends,
Gathered at the back of white folks' kitchens, and busses and
trains,

And they did tell of his feats
As their work worn hands folded laundry, tilled the land, and
birthed a nation.

And they did
Praise him for the gifts
Of pride,
Of hope,
Of honor,
He earned above ground that white men feared to tread.

Black Icarus proved his wings as strong, as steady
As any who would dare to fly.

Black Icarus passed through the gaze of the sun
When most of his brothers could not hold their heads high
enough to invite its rays upon their faces again.

Black Icarus
Whatever had been lost before him he reclaimed,
But not just for self.

When he flew, he wore the weight of his people between
those broad black shoulders.

Black Icarus climbed higher than the chains that bound them
could ever reach.

Black Icarus moved faster that the whip that oppressed them
could ever snap.

Black Icarus
Sacrificed himself to the sun to fortify the souls of his people,
Inviting them to gaze at their image burning black against its
blinding light.

Black Icarus
Then fell back to earth, his hair singed gray or gone
From his closeness to God and Heaven and Time.

Black Icarus
Stood before me,
Now, a physical slip of his legendary self.
But for the fire in his eyes, more bright from his brush with
the heavens,
I might have missed his passing.

Black Icarus
Carrying 80 plus years of life on his shoulders,
Now much more narrow than when they carried our dreams,
But they still do not bow.

Black Icarus
Draped in ceremonial armor,
The last vestment of his heavenly crusade.
The tan leather jacket, cracked and creased
Less from age than the weathering forces
It protected him,
Protected us, from.

These Tuskegee Airmen
Died by fire, if they ever truly died at all.

Black Icarus
Flew into the Sun,
Sacrificed everything
For me.

RED MAN

"Why you always want to play the Indian?"
That was always the first question.

"Ain't nobody tell you they was the bad guys?"
They used the same, tired arguments, but I never listened.

And, "How come you never want to play right?
You are supposed to die when we shoot you!"
But I didn't.

See, it was just a game of Cowboys and Indians.
And we were just five or six years old.
But I was just, single handedly, winning the wars that history
had forgot.

"We are white men with rifles!"
Bubba would scream.
"You suppose to die, when we shoot you five times!"
But I didn't.

And even with my reluctance,
They always let me play the Indian next time,
Hoping against hope I would one day accept their scripted
history.

"It didn't take John Wayne no six people to ever whup up on
one Indian."
That's what Luke would mutter with his head tied under my
arm.

But it did take five or six of them,
Black as me pretending to be
John Wayne cowboys,
to bring me down every time.

Not like in the movies at all.
I didn't like 'em and I'm not sure I was acting.

"Why you always got to be different?"
That was usually the last question.

"I don't know." I used to shrug.
"I just don't think your guns are enough to destroy me."

The funny thing is, I really didn't know.
I didn't know that my sun kissed skin had been beautifully
swirled with red as deep and dark as Georgia clay.

And in that moment, I didn't realize,
I didn't realize that I might be anything but black, no matter
my grandparents' gift,
Children of Black Feet, Crow, and Cherokee pride.

But even with all of my ignorance,
I still refused to just lie down and die for the white man.

I just hopped up on my imaginary horse,
Struck a pose, then rode off into the sunset.

And the funny thing is,
    I DIDN'T EVEN KNOW WHY.

ELTON JOHN

"Elton John IS white!
AND,
    He talk funny too."

The round brown faces surrounding me
On a hot summer day said nothing.

Some did stare unblinking
And some shook heads in disbelief
But no one actually spoke.

The truth is I was still in denial myself,
Figured I could lay it on somebody else
So, I wouldn't have to struggle alone.

See, just yesterday, I was telling my big sister,
"I'm gonna be the next Elton John when I grow up."

She paused, head cocked, then fired,
"How you gonna be the next Elton John?!?! "
She said, with a neck roll and evil grin,
"You ain't even white!"

She was already flipping through Mama's albums
When those last words dropped.

"Who got to be white?
Elton John be getting his songs played on the radio.
  Nobody said he got to be white."

Right on cue, she jerked an album from Mama's record stack,
Spun dramatically,
Shoved a picture into my face.

As my eyes adjusted,
It was right there in front of me
As plain as day.

They put a white man on Elton John's Album,

So white people wouldn't be afraid to buy it in front of they
friends.

Clear that her point had been lost on me, sister continues,
"It says here that he, Elton John, is from England."
But seeing my unchanged, blank stare, she sighed.
"How many black people you know from England?"

My glazed gaze might have made it clear
I had never imagined such a thing.
So, I just kept staring. And she kept grinning.
That's when I knew she was lying.

She expected a response,
But still looked surprised when I screamed at the top of my
lungs,
"Mama, your daughter in here telling stories again."

As mama made her way to the living room,
I snatched the album from my stunned sibling
And turned triumphantly to meet her.
"Ok Mama," I started,

"Tell my silly sister why they put this white man on Elton John's Album."

Well, as it turned out, I was educated that day.
About how not everything good in the world
Had to come from black folk,
How music was "international,"
And that Elton John...
Wasn't even the only white music we listened to.

So, there I was
On a hot summer day,
Surrounded by doubters and naysayers,
Holding an album cover
Of a white man,
In a white suit, wearing a white hat.

Well, I figured
I might as well hit them with it all at once.
So, as I pulled another album from behind my back,
I asked,

"Do y'all remember that song,
Bad, Bad Leroy Brown?"

SHE CRIES

Some nights she lies alone and cries herself to sleep
While four boys rest peacefully in the next room.

Because her oldest son, not yet twelve,
Is strong and reliable, and now the man of the house.
He will never again consider going out to play after school,
So, she cries.

Because her youngest boy reads people like blind do Braille,
And promised he would be the best President ever one day,
While bullets ring down the alley below her window,
As modern John Wilkes Booths
Frantically try to preserve their American Dream,
She cries.

Because she knows that her third boy loves science like fish
love water,
And most likely has the cure for AIDS scribbled in crayon in
his overstuffed backpack,
As junkies howl between the shattered streetlights,
Waiting to prey on those weaker than themselves,
She cries.

Because she knows her second son's command of words could
make him a New York Times Best Seller,
As somewhere a child who has never learned to read
Slips, fearfully, into an old man's fantasy,
For the promise of food and someone to hold,
She cries.

With four healthy, young, black men
Safely resting in the next room.
She lies there, trying to cry herself to sleep.

She cries because she knows.
One day soon...
    There will be only three.

HUNTING SEASON

Bernhard Goetz fired round after round
As fast as his angry little hand could squeeze the trigger.
When the smoke cleared on a crowded New York Subway,
four black males
Lay bloodying the railcar floor.

Next, Bernie calmly climbed to his feet,
Approached the one fallen nearest him,
And whispered violently,
"You don't look so bad, here's another one."

Then, he fired one last bullet
Into the shaking frame
Of somebody's lost boy.

Eyewitness reports
Cited a series of cheers…
Maybe a high-five or two.

And as the blood of four children
Began to stain the boxcar
Like all the other ignored graffiti,
A reasonable man pocketed a gun
Then calmly returned to his seat.

So, at the trial of Bernie,
It was revealed that these four black males
Were intent on robbing him that day.

Bernie admits that he had only been approached by one,
Who asked for, but never demanded, money.

Also, at Bernie's trial
It was made clear that each of these young black men
Had extensive police records.
But, as Bernie himself testified
He had no way of knowing that.

Later, it was proven at the trial of Bernie
That two of these menacing blacks carried hidden screwdrivers
Which, if wielded as weapons, could easily
Put a rational, grown white man in fear of his life.

But again, Bernie tried to be clear:
He had no idea that there were any weapons.

All Bernie knew about these four was
They were black, and
They were male, and
They looked just like the niggers
That beat and embarrassed him when he was younger.

So, when Bernie saw that look in their eyes,
You know?
That feral,
Super-Predator,
Lock up your daughters
Cause we can't help ourselves, look.

Well, when he saw whatever he needed to see,
He did what he believed any

God fearing, rational white man
Would be compelled to do.

He drew an illegal pistol and
Tried his best to shoot them dead.

When the first round exited the chamber
Bernie Getz declared,

"The life of a black man still has no value in America!"

With the first not guilty verdict
The Nation declared,

"You Go Bernie!"

When he squeezed the trigger the second time
Bernie proclaimed,

"You niggers don't have the right to commit crimes
Before justice is served."

With the second acclamation of not guilty
The World proclaimed,

"You tell them, Bernie!"

With the third and fourth bullets
Bernie screamed,
"You boy, are public enemy number one.
A side-ways look is still all I need
To string your black ass up in public."

And with the third and fourth acquittal
Someone raised their voice to God and said,

"Amen."

Then, as that final bullet lodged itself in the spine of a child,
Bernie announced,
"You, young black man, are not protected!
No matter where you go, you shall know no peace,
No matter what you accomplish, you will taste no justice."

And with a final exoneration
By a righteous jury of his peers,
A second cheer went up across this land of the free
So loud, and piercing, few could actually hear it.

But those more sensitive to the approaching storm,
We heard the announcement made coast to coast
As Bernie strolled back out the halls of his justice,
The commentator began.
"Ladies and gentlemen" he said, clearing his throat.
    "This just in, The Hunting Season has begun."

INJUSTICE

A cold December and finals are done.
Just a few hours ride and I'm home to the ones
Whose love I don't have to justify,
Whose respect I don't need to earn.

But the greyhound is late
For our midnight run.
Locked the doors at eleven,
No bus until one.

So, I sit in the cold
On my duffle, lean hard
With only this coat and
My thought to guard
Me from the winds
And blistering snow.

So, I close my eyes,
Picture myself in that place
Where I am surrounded by…

So, I close my eyes,
Picture myself in that place
Where I am surrounded by...

When I open my eyes
I am surrounded by
Squealing tires on concrete.
Blue lights flash on red

While sirens set the beat.

First one from across the lot
Then two from the left to block
Last three, swing right, and now
I am completely removed
From the watching crowd.

They begin to pile out,
These blue clowns on parade,
To serve and protect.
They start their crusade.

But as they circle, I remember
What dad used to say:
"These three rules you must learn
For your survival each day."

With their hands on batons,
White teeth are clenched tight.
Fingers start dancing on triggers
Under blinding streetlights.

"Stay calm!"
A voice echoes
In the back of my head

"Stay low!
Stand tall, son,
Then you're already dead."

"Stay alive!"

That's the lesson
I was taught at the age of thirteen.
"Learn to bottle your rage,
However wrong it may seem."

I manage a polite smile
Ask, "Is something amiss,
A small problem perhaps
I can help you all with?"

Well, that caught them off guard.
Too many words came out right.
They heard no sarcasm
Or outrage…

In spite of the obvious wrong,
In our current circumstance
They justified the scene
With a quick song and dance.

The lead cop was a pro,
Caught his balance and said,
"We had a call, just came in.
They thought someone was dead."

So, it seemed they did rush
To help their fallen fellow man
Who might have need of assistance
From their firm steady hand.

"Well, I am just fine,
In this cold I do swear!

I'm just waiting for the bus like
Those good folks, over there."

So, they hovered and circled,
Confused, in dismay,
Not sure what to do
Or quite sure what to say.

"What now?" asked the rookie.
"We're not just going to leave?"

"We must," whispered top cop.
"He won't react like we need."

So finally departing,
Each cop took his go
With a glare at me leaning
On my bag, in the snow

As the last spotlight dimmed,
I close my eyes tight
To hold back frozen tears
And thank dad for advice.

So, I whisper, again
Sure not to forget
Cause one cop's still on the lot,
And no bus has come yet.

"Stay calm,
No matter how right you are son."

"Stay low,
Don't move fast, because they will go for that gun."

"Stay alive,"
The last lesson,
"Guard the pride in your eyes.
When you're finally home safe,
You can scream, shout or cry
    At this Injustice."

TOKEN VILLANELLE

This pisses me off to no end--
I mean, the nerve it took to say,
"We already have a good black friend."

As if I was the tail of a popular trend,
They hinted that I be on my way.
This pissed me off to no end.

I did not expect to have to contend
With "Don't think we're racist when we say,
We already have a good black friend."

Their words they started to defend.
"It's just the game we were raised to play."
And it pissed me off to no end

To think, they thought this would not offend
If they warned me right away,
"We already have a good black friend."

It seemed an idea they could not transcend
They allowed the bridge to give way
And it pissed me off to the very end.
But I think they had more than they deserved
If they truly had one good black friend.

THIS POEM

This poem is for those who led the charge,
Who came up kicking and went down hard.
These words are for all the look like me's
That our history books have refused to see.

I write these words for Stagecoach Mary
Whose everyday life was twice as scary.
Black and female she took a chance
Delivering US Mail 'cross frontier land.

And what about Ms. Harriet T.
Who gave us the choice, live slave or die free!
For those that believed she had God on her side
And those that refuse... met her old .45.

This poem is for taking it to the streets
From Haiti to Selma to Georgia's Peach,
For all the Nat's from Turner to Love,
Who strapped on guns and took off gloves.

Whether revolting against old England's crown,
Or the tumbling of old Nazi town,
They stood in the flames of bigoted fear
And proved our worth to stand tall here.

We now know of legends in whispered words,
These deeds so great but seldom heard,
Praises sung so loud for fights well won
But quickly forgot once the job was done.

So, I praise Joe Louis, for sticking it to the man
The brown shirts, the Nazi's and the ku klux klan
For forcing his country to choose a side.
Do you carry more hatred, or patriot pride?

This is for the Buffalo Soldier, Dreadlock Rasta,
Riding head long into footnotes of history books,
For the promise of a "whites only" sleeping car,
For the gratitude of a lynch mob's welcome home.

What about those airmen of Tuskegee pride,
Who shot out the lights from unfriendly skies?
They danced with the devil and copped a good feel.
They showed their true mettle and strength of will.

This poem has only just begun to
Highlight the battles fought and won
By selfless gifts and sacrifice,
By the severely wronged who still chose right.

Like Peter Salem, and Salem Poor,
Two black men who served in America's first war.
At Bunker Hill when all seemed lost,
They served with distinction.
They paid the cost.

But as a new nation awoke as the land of the free,
There was no room for heroes that looked like me.
So erased from history they protected the lie
That only white folks been brave enough to die
For these dreams.

And when York traveled out with Lewis and Clark
Four thousand miles, he did his part.
Started out enslaved across this land,
But through courage and deed proved as much a man.
When indigenous people saw that black skin
Claimed that God had blessed them with Big Medicine.
But when the mission returned to these lands, "civilized,"
Ordered NOT to raise his head with pride.
No money earned, no land his to take
In gratitude for his part to make
This one united nation.

Have you ever heard of Cropperville
Down south in Missouri's old boot heel,
Where black and white Men and Women were slaved
And worked into an early grave?
But there was one who climbed his way up
With a wife and fifteen children, but

Knew that if he just walked away
No justice would ever come the Cropper's way.

So, Owen Whitfield turned round again,
Marched back into the lion's den.

He hid out the day and lived out the nights
Preaching and teaching the Croppers their rights
Saying, "there no color of child on this earth
Don't deserve to know God's grace and life's worth.
All people deserve what they hard work is due,
And if you can't be heard I will speak up for you."

Yeah, this poem is for all of the "look like me's"
Who have helped me raise my eyes to see,
To hold head high and wear skin proud,
To stare too long and laugh too loud.

But this poem has only just begun
To shine the lights and bang the drums.
It would have to last one thousand years
To begin to tell our story here.

So, I leave to you the final lines
To explore and write in your own time.
But know you this,
Whether young or old,
These are the stories
That must be told.

An important piece
To the puzzle you see
That proves this great nation
The land of the free.

So, let's continue to speak of the "look like me's"
Until our history books find the courage to see
That leaving half of a great story untold
Is an affront, a disgrace to America's brave and bold.

FIHANKRA

In the distance,
Further East than my imagination has ever dreamed,
Drummers strike chords in my heart
That have never reached these ears.

"Fihankra," the rhythm cries.
"Our good-byes were not complete."

From slave pits off the coast of Ghana.
To holding pens built and run
By traders far darker than me
The echoes of past nightmares beg forgiveness.

"Fihankra," they wail.
"Our good-byes were not complete."

An apology has been offered up to me
More public and sincere than any I have ever considered,
Even though they no longer know me.

"Fihankra," they sing
"Our good-byes were not complete."

In Ghana, today there is a movement
To wash hands, wash hearts,
Wash souls clean of a tragic miscalculation.

"Fihankra," they call.
"Our good-byes were not complete."

When they sold me
To those who were like them only in form,
Not substance, or culture, or color, not like me,
They did not realize (or perhaps even care)
How different our lives would become.

"Fihankra," they plead.
"Our good-byes were not complete."

And into the flesh burdened bellies of great galleys
They fed us over, body and soul, then watched
from the shores as we set sail for new lands.

They counted their baubles and cowry,
Not knowing that "slave" carried a more permanent meaning
To those who sheltered themselves from the sun.

Now
"Fihankra," they say,
"Our good-byes were not complete."

SOUTHERN BROTHER

He arrives at the corner
In the strokes between dawn and daylight
In rain,
In cold,
In heat
He stands, waiting to be seen
For more than the cheap labor
His work worn hands have earned
Making America great.

And I do see him
My lost brother of the southern world.

For him,
Long gone are the dreams
Of building great temples and grand avenues
In the name of gods and kings.

Replaced with hopeless hope,
More menial labor,
Less supporting pay,
If they actually pay at all.

Because like other casualties of the slaver's world,
There are few voices that will champion him in the light of day.

I watch, as a truck approaches,
Slow and deliberate,
No lights to break the last darkness

That settles the world and,
The cold hearts of God-fearing men.

"Go home or we'll send you to hell!"
A well-manicured voice fires
From the safety of tinted windows.

But my brother hardly stirs,
Just back a step, and
I catch a knowing stare,

As if to confirm
He has returned to his home
And to hell
In the same footsteps.

I want to reconcile our forced war of poverty,
Black and brown facing off like
There is a prize for being next to last.

But the newspapers fuel the fears,
And the patriot guard fuel the hate,
And the politicians fuel the lies,

All refusing to allow
A real alliance to birth itself.

So, I just keep watch from my own space,
And I just wait for the right time
When I can finally muster the audacity to lift his heart.

And I hope that

By that time
He can look into my eyes
And see how strong
We could be together.

And I hope that
By that time
I can look into his eyes
And we will be
That strong together.

But for now
He just arrives at the corner
On the strokes between dawn and daylight
In rain,
In cold,
In heat.
He is waiting to be seen
…And I do see him.

SORCEROUS EVIL

They say they don't believe in supernatural
Then gather behind high guarded walls with iron gates
In sacred covens and cabals,
Like modern living communities.

Then, like warlocks and witches before the hoary brew pot,
They begin to chant ancient incantations
Conjuring monsters to frighten the least faithful.

"Niggers are!!!"
The first summoner starts
Then attaches several adjectives to the word.
With venom enough to stand alone,
It becomes a mortal threat to the unenlightened.

The second, an enchantress
With grand gesture generates waves of primal hate,
Infuse the invocation with provocative words
Like Savage, Inhuman, Bestial, Impure
Before casting it out upon the young women
Who have refused to join in the séance.

And it is absorbed…
Gradually…
Upon contact
So, as they begin to walk their separate paths
They still, sometimes without knowing,
Clutch purses more close to heaving breast,
And sometimes without thinking

They grow fearful that feminine whiteness
May create a scent this fabricated super-predator cannot resist.

Meanwhile, the elders of the gathered,
All men of course,
Return to weaving their spell of horror,
Continue stirring their young boys to fevered action.

They simmer the words in ideas of
Superiority born of God
And their rightful place
At the front and top of the world.

Oddly they speak of birthright,
But not sacrifice,
Espouse high praise,
But not hard work.
Then, wound up like toy soldiers,
They send these children out
To shred the dreams of their neighbors.

I know
They say they don't believe in the supernatural,
But if you listen, you can still hear them
Petitioning demons from the inferno for aid.
And, if you are watching, you can still see them continue
Begging Satan himself to lie
As he whispers the devil's words,
Words like separation and loathing,
Hate and fear,
Delivered to them, as per the contract,
With an angelic voice.

So, self-deceived, they can still close their prayers
With a heartfelt "Amen."

But as they rise once more from the smoking pews,
It is clear to those still watching how completely untouched
they are
By the true glory of God.

VISIONS

The bat fell fast across my back...
The bat fell hard across my head...
The bat fell fast and hard
Across my back and head.

My vision blurred... then focused,
Blurred then focused,
On the object of my pain and fears.

I wake, trembling, lying in a pool of sweat.
The television is the source of my pain,
Brought to me in living color.

Somewhere, a black boy
Is being beaten or choked or shot or tased to death again,
And no one seems to give a damn.

Somewhere, another white man
Lies bruised and bloodied and battered in the name of some
obscene justice.

These are the images that introduce us to a "new world order."
Two steps forward and three steps back!
Our great ideas may not survive such a storm!

Somewhere, stereotypes are passed to an innocent child
Who has never seen me before,
A belief in the natural ignorance of color!

A belief that justice is and should be based on shades of darkness.

Somewhere a child like me
Who grew up tired and hungry on these streets
Has had his greatest fear come to life.
The fear that his pain matters less than any other's,
The fear that his struggle for equality
Guarantees him no respect.

Somewhere our children,
Black and White,
Native and Immigrant,
Have been led to ruin
Because justice has turned a blinded eye upon their tears.

With these thoughts to torment me,
I drift painfully back to sleep.
But in this dream,
There is a weapon in my hands

And in this dream
There is a confused white man
Chained and thrown at my feet.
And in this dream,
He starts to curse me.
He starts to goad me into what he knows
Must be my next act.

But he looks surprised
As I raise the weapon high above my head
And bring it down

Against the chains that have held us ignorant for so long.
Then I extend my hand to him.

So now as we start our journey
Toward understanding
He will learn that he can rest his tired weight on strong black
shoulders.

So now as we start our trek
Toward the truth,
I will learn that I can trust blue eyes to watch my back.

And now as we start our pilgrimage
Towards unity,
We will learn that justice is still alive.

We will learn that Just Us few people
Have always had the power to restore this beauty's righteous
sight.

Now these are my visions
For all of you…
My People.

book two

as my God lay sleeping

I tremble for my country when I reflect that God is just: that his justice cannot sleep forever... The Almighty has no attribute which can take side with us...

- Thomas Jefferson (1854).

"The writings of Thomas Jefferson: being his autobiography, correspondence, reports, messages, addresses, and other writings, official and private," p.404

AS MY GOD LAY SLEEPING

As my God lay sleeping
Europe proclaimed itself
Lord of the Universe
In her name,

Then set about destroying the artifacts of any culture that could
challenge that claim.

And while His story was re-written a thousand times,
My contributions always fell on the cutting room floor.

As my God lay sleeping
I, once a great hunter, became the hunted.
Like prey tracked across the Savannah, along the Coast,
Then delivered into the hands of "God's Chosen,"
Most times by those with skin darker than mine.

As my God lay sleeping
A good Christian beat me,
Carved the word SLAVE into my back,
Then invited others to poke and prod me
Like a prized bull on the block.

And I bit my lip
As whips and chains ground marks in my skin,
And I calculated my survival,
So that others could learn of revolution.

As my God lay sleeping
Our founding fathers,
And you know exactly what I mean,
Penned hollow words of liberation.
"We hold these truths to be self-evident,
That all men are created equal."
But to insure there was no confusion
I was quickly declared a savage.
They tried to legislate only three fifths of my humanity.

As my God lay sleeping
A man proclaimed himself my master,
Explained it was his duty to punish me,
Said this was my only path to salvation,
And, if I stopped being a troublesome nigger
His God would make me a house slave in the next kingdom.
That same man seemed completely surprised
When I burned his plantation,
Then delivered him up to his God
With the same dull knife that he used to castrate me.

As my God lay sleeping
The brand of predator was seared into my blistering existence.
Charged with the rape of white purity,
No one would question their blinding fear
So, once again I became hunted.
Leaving my mothers and sisters to bravely fight alone,
Waiting to be desecrated by the loveless souls of Christian
virtue.

As my God lay sleeping
This hunt continued for sport.

And while tied like a sacrificial hog,
I recognized the sheriff that arrested me.
As rope was tossed over a sturdy oak,
My attorney who put up no defense spat in my face.
As the last breath ebbed from my dangling consciousness,
I could make out the judge, in the robes of his absolute authority.
He threw the first burning bottle at my feet,
Commanded it shatter upon kindling so carefully placed.

As my God lay sleeping
I went to war against an enemy that was never mine,
Faithfully killed any who dared rebel against the American icon: freedom.
While at home,
The rapes of my mother continued,
And in the streets,
The assassinations of my father intensified,
And in the woods
The emasculated screams of my brother shattered the darkness,
And in my nightmares
My sisters began to fear what I became to protect their American dream.

As my God lay sleeping
I was fooled into believing
That the blood of my brothers
Was worth less than that of others.
So, I killed once, then again,
"Just one mo' dead nigger," said the cop who released me.
"You just saved me a bullet."

But, when I drew white blood, again I was hunted,
This time like a feral animal,
A menace to society.

As my God lay sleeping
I was beaten nearly to death by a lynch mob wearing badges,
They swore to protect and serve, but the duty,
It seems, was not promised to me.
Although it was not my first beating, this time there was proof,
But the world, so thoroughly disgusted with what they had
seen,
Condemned me for opening their eyes.

As my God lay sleeping
A white woman strapped her two baby boys into their car seats.
Then, in an act of cold-blooded murder,
She drove her car, with her children, seats and all, into a lake.
Then she casually walked away.
She did not run for cover,
She didn't hide out the days.
She wasn't even afraid to show her face.
Because she knew, just like you know
That racism and hatred had seeped so deep into prime time,
Had created a super predator to blame for her crime.

I peered out of my window,
As this murderer described her monster
And sadly, was not surprised that it looked like me,

I locked my car doors,
As the world listened without doubt.
"It's a wonder he didn't rape her first,"

Some old man whispers, staring through me as I pass.
"You can dress 'em up but they still savages."

And again, I became the main attraction
At a lynching in my honor,
Hosted this time by the media,
For the entire world to witness.

But strangely, no apology was forth coming
When the truth was revealed.
No retractions were made when the evidence was clear.
Just the occasional, "Hell, it doesn't mean they wouldn't have done it,
If we gave them half a chance."

As my God lay sleeping
Soap Operas coast to coast were interrupted with horrible news.
"A poor child was caught in a deadly crossfire, a gang shoot-out."
Again, the nation's righteous condemnation soared,
Demanded justice from the monsters
That would harm one golden strand on that poor angel's head.

But for the third time this week
I cradle the riddled remains of a child with kinky black hair.
I sit waiting for a sign of public outcry.
I focus my eyes so that I can see the angry mob approach
I rock back and forth ready to pass on the world's heartfelt sympathy,

But they do not reach me.

They never reach me.
And again, I am here, alone, to throw dirt into the mass grave
That has formed beneath our shared existence.

As my God lay sleeping
I gather the tattered and scarred remains of my humanity.
Finding a jagged stick, I dip it into my exposed veins.
And begin to chronicle the events of this Un-Civil War.
So that when My God once again
Takes note of this world gone mad,
She will know
The true nature of those
Claimed to act on His words.

But as my God lay sleeping
I continue my vigilant witness,
Ensuring injustice will not thrive unchallenged.

MY STREET

Bullets fell like rain last night on my street.
Chaos laughed,
Vile tongue lapping at the festering humanity
Spilled around us.

Another child was laid to rest on concrete
As tearful mothers cried the ritual cry.
Name after name they called,
Afraid, panicked, hopeless.

Their chorus did little to comfort them,
Cause like every other night,
One did embrace the cold arms of despair.
And the rest?
They pray themselves to sleep
Then dream in fear of what tomorrow night will bring.

But any questions will go unanswered
Because blood does not stain concrete,
And only a mother could remember his good deeds.

See, you're automatically a gangster,
If you're born on my street.
Here bullets fall like rain on concrete.

Dark hearts taunt the chalk souls that map the ground
As our children bear witness to their future
The Devil grinds his teeth, flashes an evil grin,

Counts the hours back
Until he can once again drink
In the pain of a young mother's tears.

So as bullets continue to fall like rain,
Chaos laughs,
And humanity gathers in small puddles along my street.
Then slowly...
        Drains away...

THE UNCIVIL WAR

The uncivil war will not be televised,
The uncivil war will not be televised,
The uncivil war will not be televised,
But it will be brought to you In Living Color.

A commentator near the scene of the first official skirmish
Noted the screams of children wasting away seemed so real,
She almost turned her head.
"Their starving bellies were close to popping," she reported.
"It was hard to imagine this scene in America, and I,
I almost felt responsible for their pain torn lives…
Almost."

The uncivil war will not be televised,
The uncivil war will not be televised,
The uncivil war will not be televised,
But you can catch it on Live Stream
At www.kill-d-killers.com

SEE!
Masked troops in Government Issue splatter guards
Open fire on pregnant women outside abortion clinics!
Hear!
Officers wielding righteous accents explain, "The best way to preserve the rights of these unborn Americans who might never have the chance to suffer inadequate education, declining family assistance, poor housing prospects, and extended incarceration as the workforce of a major corporation… Well, the best way to preserve our dreams for

those youngsters is to put a bullet through the head of old mommy dearest. "I mean, after all we're not called pro-lifers for nothing."

The uncivil war will not be televised
The uncivil war will not be televised
The uncivil war will not be televised
But you can catch the special holiday program
Live on pay per view

"With late breaking news this is Wally Tsaboutime coming to you live from minority central ... where, just moments ago the special war on drug enforcement teams cleared all "civilian" traffic from this dead-end urban housing unit.
We have learned that several well to do citizens Including three doctors, two government officials and a local attorney are praising the task force for escorting them out of the maze of drug infested alleys they accidentally stumbled into at nearly three o'clock on a Sunday morning.

After these thankful pillars of the community are safe,
the task force will commit itself to an all-out assault on these enemies of the state.
They have planned for 10 young slangers
(that's street vernacular for low level, street corner, drug dealers, with no real power) to be taken out in a simultaneous sniper barrage triangulated on the corners of Malcolm X Blvd and MLK Ave.

At the same time, a 100-family tenement building
(suspected of housing a reputed crack house on one of its lower floors) will be bombed by an elite unit of light artillery

specialist on loan from an unspecified allied nation.

The precision strike will destroy the structural integrity of the 5-story building, bringing it straight down, expecting no significant inconvenience to the good citizens of highly gentrified communities that surround it.

A spokesperson says "it will be several days before we can accurately disclose how many of these and I quote "reality dodging, dead end job working no prospect having scum we obliterated today." End quote

That's ok Officer, cause we law-abiding citizens know that every little bit helps.

The uncivil war will not be televised,
The uncivil war will not be televised,
The uncivil war will not be televised,
But you can get the highlights at noon, six, and eleven.

In a related story, a small tactical assault team has issued it's official apology for their role in an accidental raid earlier today of a Spanish speaking Church's youth bible revival. It seems that the members of the church are claiming that they had been so moved in their singing of praises to God that they failed to hear the armed men enter and order them to the floor. A rookie has been blamed for the miscommunication. In his defense he has made it clear that he thought that one of the young men who, even to us, seemed much older that 10 years old, was making a grab for what appeared to be a gun. It has not, however, yet been explained how the child was shot in the back. We got some bad intelligence, said the spokesperson for the privately owned assault team, how we suppose to know that those people would actually be in a church praying on a Wednesday night?

The uncivil war will not be televised?
The uncivil war will not be televised??
The uncivil war will not be televised???
Bullshit!!!!!
Truth is we've become fascinated by the coverage
And have become so god damn shiftless
that we thought we were doing something revolutionary
when we finally stood up
just to change the fucking channel

The uncivil war will not be televised,
The uncivil war will not be televised,
The uncivil war will not be televised,
But it will be coming soon.
          to an exclusive community near you.

BEBE'S SONG

Do you remember that song by Bill Withers?
You know, "Lean on Me":
"Sometimes in our lives
We all have pain
We all have sorrow,
But if we are wise
We know that there's always tomorrow."

Anyway, that was the song playing on the radio
The day I got the news.

See, I was at home by myself

And I had the radio turned up kinda loud
And I guess I was trying to sing too.
Then the phone rang.

"Hello," I answered, but nobody spoke.
"Hello!!!" I said a bit louder.
And this voice starts screaming,
  "He's dead!!!
They Killed BeBe!!!!!"

Suddenly the whole world is spinning
I am trying my best to sit down before I fall,
with this voice echoing through my soul.

  "They killed BeBe."
And Bill was on the radio singing,

"Call me when you need a friend."

See, BeBe was my cousin, Cedric.
He was about the same age as my brother, Tony,
And he was dead.

He was the first of my generation to go out like that.
He wasn't the youngest, and he wasn't the last.
He just got to be the first.

BeBe was trying to be a good father at seventeen,
And he liked to run the streets… well we all ran the streets.

But he knew how to laugh at himself,
And you have to know how to laugh at yourself
If you hope to survive those St. Louis streets.

So I go home for the funeral,
And the boy who killed my cousin is already out of jail.
So, me and mine start talkin' like it's time to go play, you know?

It's time to play Judge!
It's time to play Jury!
It's time to play Executioner!

And that's when it hits me.
Hard.
This is what it's all about!

It's about letting your emotions drive you to the edge of
insanity.
It's about holding on so tight, and so long to the dumb shit

That it eats you up from the inside,
And it builds,
And it builds,
Then, BLAM…

You can't help but go off!
Just like that fuckin' gun!

As another baby sits staring at a door that she don't know will
never open again,
And another mother sits, cradling a phone that she knows will
never ring again,
A whole family and another community is changed forever,
again.

But that is not how I want to make it to the other side.
So I start trying real hard not to let other people push my
buttons,
Make me do things.

But sometimes I still get so damn mad I can't see straight.
And then that song will pop into the back of my head.

And sometimes I pick up my phone
And I push that little star button…
And I say "Hello."
You know… I'm talkin' to the other side.

I say, "I miss you BeBe,"
And, I say, "I miss you Stebo,"
Damn, I miss JoJo,
See, JoJo was only 14 years old when they shot him in the head.

I say, "I miss you," and
"I will never forget you," and
"Thanks for listening...
I wish, I wish, I wish, I could return the favor,
"But I'll talk to you again real soon.
I love you. Just keep watching my back.
Peace."

And the whole time it's that song.
See, it never stops playing in the back of my head,
 "I'm right up the road and
 I'll share that load if you just call me...
call me."

Yeah, I remember that song.
        Because now that's BeBe's song.

THE POOL

She leads them through the maze,
Housing designed to protect them from the outside world,
And save the outsiders any vision that might disrupt their
fragile truths.

They walk slowly past the pool,
Remember it once promised excitement
To hundreds on hot August days.

But today
They pass, well trained,
Take in everything,
See nothing,
Stay clear.

This pool has become a repository,
The putrid holding tank
For the discarded fragments
Of their community dreams.

The shallows now serve as huddling grounds
To people like Richard,
The one boy Miss Etta got left.
He the only person don't know he is going to die soon.
A Meth death for sure.

The deeper end is partially filled
Rancid waste that might have been water, once.
That's where Nina's childhood was taken.

Three hours of tortured baptism
With no witness to her fall from grace.

Deeper still, in that same dark water
T.C., a drug dealer, was found dead.
Two weeks later
The day after Nina's three brothers enlisted for the army.

Maybe once that pool promised excitement to
hundreds on hot August days.
But today, like every other day since,
It is just another obstacle to navigate
As she leads them through the maze of housing
Which serves to protect them from the outside
And save those outsiders
Any painful visions
        that might disrupt their frail set truths.

"Hurry Up!" I shouted as he cleared the fence.
"I ain't scerred of no dog," he snarled.
Then walked slowly toward the ball.
Screams erupt and I see it.
One hundred pounds of terror,
And it was all over my cousin.

I think, maybe Stebo was trying to fight it.
I think, maybe my cousin crazy.
I think, maybe that saved his life.

An uncle jumped the fence,
Attacked the beast.
A second appeared,
Cradling a bloody child,
Disappeared.
Adults are screaming,
Children crying.
Somewhere dogs are howling.

"My daddy didn't care 'bout me."
That's the first thing he says
As we start down the street.

"The only other person besides her that ever cared about me
was your mama."

Me and Stebo,
Fifteen years and one hundred stitches later,
And we still trying to get to the corner store.
I've only seen him three times since I left St. Louis.

The first was at our grandfather's funeral.
We were still young enough to not seem hard, but we already
were.

The second was a few years later at my cousin's funeral.
Shot over five dollars in a crap game,
At seventeen, BeBe proved the mortality of an entire
generation.

Stebo peaks around the corner before he turns.

"If it's something I need to know, Stebo,
You better spill now if you want backup."

He half laughs. "Nah, I'm OK man."
That's all I get before he quickly changes the subject.
"Remember when we was kids?

And your mama use to let us all sleep over,
And she would make us all the foods we liked,
And we would stay up all night?"

"Yeah." I laugh. I remember.

"Man, she was the shit...
Sometimes, I wish she could have been..."

He turns away, choking on the words, but they still hit me.

"... my mama."

Now we're awkwardly standing outside the liquor store, so
that's where we leave our conversation.

The Asian man behind the bullet proof glass watches,
Takes a mental picture... just in case.

"Gimme a forty of Malt Liquor and some chips,"
Stebo shouts through a hole in the bulletproof wall,
"And some penny candy for my nieces."
Stebo turns to me.
"Man, remember when penny candy uses to cost a penny?"

I laugh, again, realizing how long I have been gone, how much
I missed this.
We slide money through the hole in the counter,
The man turns the tray so we can get our stuff.

"Have a good day," I say. One of my new habits.
But he just looks the other way.

Now Stebo is laughing at me and peeking out the door. I start
to speak.
"You still into that Hung Kung Fuey shit?"
He cuts me off and takes a drag off a cigarette I didn't see him
light.

"Yeah, I still practice some"
I say, now anxiously looking over my shoulder.
He continues,
"I bet you can kick some ass now! I wish my mama would a
put me in something like that.
Maybe I wouldn't be so much trouble now."

A car backfires and we both react instinctively,
Stebo dives for cover, I spin toward the noise.

"I see you still run the wrong way when trouble starts,"
That's what he says from somewhere behind me.
"You know, that Boy Scout shit gonna get you killed one day,
man."

I turn to laugh just in time to see him
Put an automatic pistol back in his pocket.
I can't ask. and he won't tell.

"Maybe I can go to Atlanta with your mama when they leave,
She could straighten me up,"
He says without blinking.
"Shit, look what she did to you."
The rest of the walk is silent.
We have never been closer.

Before we reach the house
We are set upon by wild children.
"Whatchu got?"
"Can I have some?"
"Give me a sip. I ain't no punk!"
"I smoke sometimes too."
"Get that damn candy out my face."
"I ain't scerred of you."
They would have been us fifteen years ago.

But when the candy is gone so are we,
Into the house.
There the grown folks have gathered,
Where they always do.
Playing pinochle, spades or rummy, you know?
Whatever grown folks play.
Me and Stebo head for the kitchen

There we find hungry people and good food.
We got fried chicken, peach cobbler, macaroni and cheese,
Sweet potato pie, mashed potatoes, red Kool-Aid!
There is enough here to feed an army, which is good,
'Cause we soldiers now.

"Mama should be proud of this," Stebo whispers.
"Man... I hope I get a party like this, when I die."

We walk to the back yard in silence.
Stebo pops the forty and whispers something close to a prayer,

And here comes young cousin, eyes wide open.

"Y'all gonna let me hit that?" He asks.
But We just stand there.
After a long silence Stebo closes his eyes,
Starts pouring the beer onto the ground.

"This is for my mama Elnora Lovelace," he starts.
"She had a hard life and a hard death."
He passes me the bottle.

"This is for Cedric Davis, BeBe," I tip the bottle.
"And the strong that survived him."

"This is for grandparents that we never got to know," Stebo
continues.
"This is for brotherhood that never got to grow," I add.

I can hear my cousins out in front the street, playing Double
Dutch games.

"This is for family," Stebo whispers,
Then takes a gulp from the near empty bottle.

"This is for family," I repeat, and I pass the bottle to Young
Cousin.

He looked at the bottle, smiling
Then back at me, his smile is gone.

"This is for family," he whispers.
Then, turns the bottle upside-down, empties it into the earth.

Stebo promised my mother a call.
But it never came.
Ten months later he was dead,
Dragged three blocks by two white boys in a pickup truck.
But they didn't call it a hate crime.

I heard he was trying to stop a fight
Between them and some brothers on the Southside.

All I could think of was that Boy Scout thing.

Four months later,
Stebo's baby brother JoJo was dead,
Only fourteen years old, shot in the head.

"This is for Joseph Lovelace," I start.
"I hope there was still innocence in his heart."

"This is for Steven Lovelace,
Because he earned his Badge of Honor."

"This is for Elnora Lovelace,
She had a hard life and a hard death."

"This is for Cedric Davis "BeBe",
And the strong that survived him. "

"This is for brotherhood
that never had a chance to grow."

"This is for the grandparents
we never had the chance to know."

"This is for family." I say,
Then take a big gulp,

And as I hand the bottle to Young Cousin on my right,
I realize that we have passed on tradition
That only old men should ever know.
But we do,
too well,
too soon.

"This is for family," he says
Then he empties that bottle into the earth.

NIGHTMARE

The door slams.
Angry feet lumber up the stairs
Towards my sanity.

"Open the god damn door," he howls.
"If I have to break it down,
It's coming out of your ass."

As tears fall, I reach for the door,
Hesitate,
Trying to talk myself down.

But a quick glance at the broken arm,
And two floating ribs, jab me into reality.

"I'm only going to say this one more time,"
He hisses through his clenched teeth,
"OPEN THE GOD DAMN DOOR!"

A latch turns,
Door flies
Like on those cartoons
I use to watch.

The Boone's Farm assaults me,
Even before he reaches.

Screaming something about me
Costing him his job
And the only woman he ever loved,
  Before punching me in the throat

I fall back onto his bed,

Watch him turn the last of the love potion
Into his angry heart,
Weakly begging him to leave me.

"Ain't no boy of mine gonna beg like no bitch,"
He barks, raising the bottle above his head.
Brings it down

I shake violently
Out of my sleep.
There is sweat
Where there should be blood.

So, I breathe deep.
Thank God.

And the door slams
Angry thoughts stumble up the stairs
Towards my sanity.

"Open the Goddamn door," it starts.
And I begin to pray
"Please God,
Wake me ...
Soon."

MERRY-GO-ROUND

"Angelica was just wheeled into the emergency room."
The reporter starts, "D.O.A. Dead On Arrival."
Her chart read like a grocery list,

- ✓ massive blood loss,

- ✓ sub-cranial hemorrhaging,

- ✓ epidermal lacerations,

- ✓ failed response to life-support devices.

Strange, the report held no mention of the bullet.
It entered through Angelica's head just below the ear,
Exiting through her left temple.
She didn't die instantly, mercifully.
But with her last breath she tried to tell Justin that she forgave him,
And that she was sorry for calling him a nerd.

Five minutes ago, Justin pulled the trigger, three times,
Just like the "Gang banger" did in the movie last week.
"Don't you ever call me a nerd again." he shouted as she fell
at his feet.

He didn't expect so much blood.
"I-I I told her not to tease me,"
He stuttered to the families gathered,
"Cause I know where Ricky keeps his gun."

Justin dropped the weapon,
Fell sobbing next to his best friend;

Knowing, maybe for the first time,
This was not like the movies,
He would never see Angelica smile again.

Five Hours ago
Ricky reached into the closet for an overdue library book,
He didn't notice the laundry basket turned upside down.
He failed to see the gun his "friend" gave him was missing.

Until last week most of Ricky's classmates called him a nerd.
That changed when he pulled the gun Carlos gave him.
Even the bullies that teased and beat him respected the gun.

Ricky didn't use it. He wasn't sure it was even loaded.
So he hid it high in the closet, where his little brother Justin
could never reach.

Five days ago
Carlos watched a grown man tug at his pant leg.
"Give me another rock; I swear I'll have all your money in two days,
I got to feed my family with thi. . ."
BLAM, BLAM, BLAM

Carlos fired three shots; Henry owed three hundred dollars.
"If you don't have my money, don't taste my honey."
Carlos laughed at the irony; Henry gave him the gun last week.

Ricky, the boy who tutored Carlos until he dropped out of
school last year, was being bullied.
He gave Ricky the gun for protection.
Besides, who keeps a murder weapon lying around?

Five weeks ago
Henry entered through the basement.
When the family went on vacation
They requested their paper delivery suspended.

"I'll place the request myself," said Henry.
"You folks have a swell vacation, Mr. McDaniels."

Crawling through the McDaniel's house,
Henry had forgotten his own family days ago.
The gun he found was nice.
Maybe it's a collector's item, he thought.
Carlos might let me go another week for this.
Henry left the McDaniel's house a mess, forgot to cancel their
paper and never returned to work.

Five months ago
James McDaniel bought a gun for Daryl's 10th birthday.
The flea market had a good deal; no registration, no tax.

While inspecting the piece a young girl watched.
"Why do people buy guns if they are so bad?"
Angelica blurted before her mother could shush her.

James smiled.
"Guns only hurt bad people honey," he said.
"I don't think you'll ever have to worry about 'em."
James was still smiling at his great answer, when he laid the
cash on the table.

When the gun was stolen four months later,
James never reported it. "It wasn't registered" he said,

"It's not like they'll ever find it."

Five seconds ago
        The reporter started,
"Miguel was wheeled into the emergency room,
Pronounced Dead On Arrival."
His chart reads like a grocery list:

- ✓ massive blood loss,

- ✓ sub-cranial hemorrhaging,

- ✓ epidermal lacerations,

- ✓ failed response to life-support devices.

Strange, the report holds no mention of the bullet.
It entered through Miguel's chest just below his heart,
Exiting through his left collar bone.
He didn't die instantly, mercifully.
So, with his last breath he tried to tell Sarah
How sorry he was for sneaking to the playground after dark
For one last spin on the
Merry-go-round ride.

HUMPY TRUMP.D

Humpy Trump.D promised a wall,
Trump.D said it'd be ready by fall.
And "although Mexico will foot the bill
Congress should authorize spending, still."

Humpy Trump.D could
Swing a club,
Tie his shoes,
And bite some heads.

Humpy Trump.D could
Speak in code,
Start some fights,
Over things he misled.

But Trump.D says there is a way.
Just you listen close to what he say.
A way to infer, 'cause he thinks we're all dumb
He can convince us still, that he is the one
To keep us safe and save our dough.
Then talk to God and truly know
The evil of men and heathen cults
That sit and plot to blow us up.

Humpy Trump.D
Could split our house,
And tells some lies
Then poses with Russia
As our nation divides.

Then Trump.D screams,
"America First!"
On Sweatshop swag from China's worst

Then Trump.D filed bankruptcy, again
And blamed bad business laws for all his sins.

But, Trump.D says that **white** makes right…
No, Trump.D says that **might** makes right…
I mean Trump.D says **the right** makes rights.

Shit!

King Trump.D says he gets hoppin' ass mad
At all these god damn liberals and fags
Trying to ruin his perfect plan
To focus a nation on just one man.

Trump.D say he'll be damned and delivered
If he can't outdo one sorry sand nigger,
This Barack Bin Laden Obama Hussein.
Hell, he's seen the birth certificate.
He just won't read the damn name.

Out there waging a war
Against secular sin,

After living in excess
On whiskey and gin,

Being sheltered by power
And political might,

Thinks he can bully the world ,
Like making war is his right.

Holy wars ordained by God
While casting down women
who want to have jobs,

Killing hopes and slaying dreams,
All the while supporting the team

Of industrialists,
Cause they're serving up oil,
And to those who support them
Go the spoils ... of this war.

...Uhmmmm

Trump.D says when he starts to shout,
He sometimes forget who he's talking about.

But don't be fake newsed,
Or under re-stood.
Outside of being rich,
He T-Dawg, from the "hood."

He been where you at,
Likes to give a shout out,
Got high def in his ride
And gold fonts in his mouth.

Black gold, Texas T!

Well, the next thing you know
Trump's a millionaire again,
His college belly up,
But thanks to Fox and Friends,
He's had a new man crush,
And Bannon was his name.
So they moved to old DC
To flush the country down the drain

Trump.D says that it's no use
To keep asking him about the truth,
Cause the truth is in the mouth
Of the president ...
NOT the house...

He says low expectations are the rage
Y'all don't need no Goddamn living wage,
Because these women too bossy
Like Hillary B.
And blacks getting too proud
To just wait and see.
These damn poor getting all uppity
And the gays going straight
To the top of Trump Towers to copulate.

And if worse comes to worse, ya'll refuse to give in,
Well, he'll just grant himself more power
then bash your heads in.

King Trump.D says, "When the world judges me,
I'm gonna put it on Twitter for you all to see"
Who was on God's side and who had the orders

To send more American children to slaughter.
For their sins against us those heathens must die.
Any heathen will do, so I won't specify.

And no matter how many I send to their death
 It is a small price to pay to keep all the wealth
In the hands of a few who know
That damned American Dream speech
Was just meant for show.
But Humpy Trump.D could strike a chord
And bang a drum
And draw lines in the sand.

Humpy Trump.D could strut around
And play the clown
And make demands.

And Trump.D says,
"You don't like what you see?
Then stand up and speak…
The constitution says you're free."

Just don't be surprised if the job is lost.
And when your house is burning down,
Remember the cost
Of safety for you in these dangerous times
Where speaking the truth might just blow your damn mind.

So, Trump.D says, "Don't stir up dust.
We have ways of finding those we distrust.
Just cast out your doubt
And join my crusade

Cause the life you have
Might be the first one you save."

Humpy Trump.D will swing a club
And tie his shoes
And bite some heads.

Humpy Trump.D will tell some lies
And pick some fights
And make things dead.

book three

where hope trumps fear

WHEN MALCOLM DANCED

When Malcolm Danced
The world sauntered after him like fretful grandmothers.
Bears on bicycles veered from their paths
To clear the way for his highly interpretive life movement.

On sturdy legs that would have been tree trunks
Had he been born a sapling oak,
Malcolm begins to churn the earth,
Creating seismic rifts with each beat, beat, beat,
The driving rhythm of his heart.

When Malcolm danced there was
A move, pause, move, move, pause cadence,
Closely resembling the breaking stride of gazelles,
And his feet seemed at least as sure.

When Malcolm danced
I saw in him everything I had longed for
But never had the courage to dream of.

When Malcolm danced
My racing blood finally began to calm
To the pumping of his heart and legs.

Then, when my breathing returned to normal,
I pressed record and prayed he would dance eternity away
In the recess' of my aging soul.

ACES

He looked into my face, his one good eye dancing
In the confusion that were his thoughts.
"Told ja I ca fly," he said,
Then coughed up something unrecognizable.
"I am a pilot. See."

I know the old man with an unnatural curve in his back
From sleeping in cans and hiding in doorways
Wasn't even forty-five.

He removed an iron cross, with tattered ribbons
From a hole in his outer layer of clothing.
"My secret pocket," he whispered.

Sure, Ace, as he liked me to call him,
Could remember the war
Like it was yesterday,
'Cause that was the day that he became MIA.
Missing In America.

It is a post-war condition that captured so many
Who gave more than they had volunteered.

Many return mentally or socially bankrupt.
Ace was just another example
The American dream turned nightmare.

"T-Th-Thanks for the 'mergency fuel part'na," he stuttered,
            then slurped the last bowl of cold soup down.
"I got me a stealph mission t'nite,
 But I'll be alright.
An' iffin you hear from Uncle Sam
Tell 'im I think I'm ret to go home . . .
. . . If they don't need me no more I mean."

A pause
"Soons I gits the thumbs up . . ."

He turned back into the darkness that was the city around us,
". . . I'll be ret to go."

Pulling his goggles down, he looked back over his shoulder.
"Tell 'em, as long as they keep that light burning
I'll find a way home!
Don't y'all warry bout me.

I'm American made boy,
Dependable and strong,
I'm always gonna find a way home."

As he spread his arms
And glided into the darkness
He repeated his promise
"I'm always gonna find my way home."

With that he disappeared.
And, standing in the darkness, I whispered a short prayer for
his fading words.
Then, I reached up, turned on my porch light,
Because, I mean, who really knows?
How many more aces we got out there, running low on fuel.

Maybe if I keep one more light burning
An Ace or two might recognize it in the distance,
And maybe,
One day,
They will all finally come on home.

WHEN I FIND

When I find justice
I will know her by her un-blind eyes,
I will lay before her, face down
Begging, "free my bound hands with your sword of truth,"
Then take my rightful place
In her crusade.

When I find hope
I will know him
By his shy and isolated look,
So, I will sit and speak softly to him a while
Before welcoming him
To play with the children I have been cradling in his absence.

When I find peace
I will know her
By her un-judging smile.
In her presence
I will lay down my tearful rage,
then wash her feet in preparation for our journey together.

When I find love
I will question what he did
To be banned from the "newest" versions
Of the Bible, Koran and Torah.
I will pray with him,
That these revisions
Have not been saved to our spirit drive
As NEW GOD 4.0

POWER POEM

This right here is my power poem,
And I only shout it out
When I need to make the world back up.

See my power poem is sharp like me
And with this power poem I can cut thru crap
Way before I have to start walking in it.

Sometimes I just sling my poem.
At offending ideas,
And weak-minded thoughts.
I pitch it at anything and everything
That tries to keep me in my place.

I just launch it
With all my wit,
Straight slashing that trash talk
With my verbal accuracy.

See, this power poem is not your
Garden variety, run-of-the-mill, everyday power poem.
It is not power poem lite
Or one calorie power poem.
It ain't a decaf power poem with just a hint of hazelnut.

This power poem contains 100%, High octane, super-
caffeinated, un-filtered might!

It's the kind of poem that can make a mama's boy

Leave home, start cooking, get a job, make the bed, and wash
his own stank draws.

It's the kind of poem that will make that dog you always see
chasing cars,
Come walking home with a tire.

It's the kind of poem
That could make a woman want to bring home the bacon,
Fry it up in the pan and eat the whole damn meal herself,
Then tell her man that if he was really hungry,
Dinner would have been ready when she hit the door.

Oh yes this is a power-full poem.
And in case you still have doubt,
I am serving up free samples just for you,
And you,
And you.

So, open up your ears
Cause when the first verse caresses your brain ...

Damn!

You won't be able to just sit around
And wait for the world to get right.

You are gonna feel the urge to grab this baby by the love
handles and turn it upside down all by yourself.

See, this right here is my power poem
And I only whip it out when the world needs to recognize.

Then just like Batman
I disappear into the night
Leaving only these words
Stuck like blades in the back of your mind.

THROUGH HIM

He descended out of dreams
Of what fatherhood could be,
Should be, would be, if it was right,
If there was a God.

Draped in the warrior's garb of two worlds,
Urban guerrilla, jungle commando,
He showed me that black was just a color,
But was an important color because I wore it,
If nothing else.

When I was old enough to act like a man,
He showed me what a man was supposed to be.
He loved my mama and her children
Like we were his own,
Because he said we were.

When I was older
He taught me of revolution and causes.
"Stand for what you believe,
Die for what you deserve."

That's what he said to me,
Although the words never passed is lips.

Through him
I became a Black Panther
Stalking the landscape of my urban jungle,
Looking for the beast bold enough to face me down.

Through him
I became the child chief
Leading my clan into the unknown.

Through him I became a man.

YOU MY BROTHER

Yesterday
In the back woods of Kentucky
Or Alabama or Georgia,
We ran hard on the heels of freedom.
The hounds of Hell tracked us, by scent
Or fearful determination.

"We gonna have to jump for it."
His words explode between short breaths,
Even as he speeds to a mad man's sprint.
"We can only make it or die, either way we free."

Without pause he launched himself,
Took flight,
Landed gracefully more than twenty feet away.

Then I, with legs much weaker
Than my heart was determined,
Threw myself behind him,
Heard the cracking ribs,
Felt the sharp jagged rocks, and
Slowly began my descent into freedom.

In defiance of barking dogs and rifles,
I shook my fist one last time at the world
And found him reaching
From the edge of the abyss.

Air escaped a punctured lung,

Eyes begged him.
Leave. . .
Live. . .
For both of us.

"You ain't too heavy," he growled
 Beneath the strain of my weight
And his beating heart.
"You, my brother."

Today
He is Guardian Angel
And I am guarding his back
When he falls to winter's vicious bite.

I find him, face down, surrounded by his faithful lieutenants.
He refuses my aid,
Begs me to safeguard his soldiers first
And in the minute it takes me to return,
I am nearly a minute too late.

He, dancing between the light
And the warm embrace of forever,
Questions my decision to return.

"You ain't too heavy,"
I scream over the rush of fear
That makes his frozen body warm by comparison.
"You are my brother."

Yesterday
I dangled by my neck

Beneath the trees which bare the strangest fruit
Where the lynch mobs gather to harvest weekly.

In a brief moment of consciousness
I hear them clearly, Hells Hounds still hunt the Gemini,
My brother in soul.

Then, like Gibraltar
A sturdy rock rises beneath me
Loosens death's grip on my soul.
And without missing a beat,
Loads the last shell into an old Henry rifle.

As the predators circle,
He is now unable to clearly fight
Or save me at the same time.

"Get on boy," I whisper.
"You only gonna kill us both if you stay."
But my foundation never faltered.

"You ain't too heavy," he roared,
Then gazed down the barrel straight into the gates of Hell.
"You, my brother."

Today
We are surrounded by cops on a street corner.
His lungs and heart have stopped,
So, mine is trying like hell
To beat for both of us.

"Our protectors" don't pretend to offer assistance

But are quick to throw in sage advice.
"I don't think you gonna be able to save this one."
One spits, "You just pushing dead weight boy."

"He ain't too heavy,"
 I shout through angry eyes,
As hands that have been trained to kill
Find more important hearts to hold . . . to pound.
"He's my brother."

And, tomorrow
I will peer at him through chain link and razor mesh,
Try to hold tight through this wire thin connection
And a few dollars for deodorant.

He will hint that he feels himself
A burden on my heart and new family, my new life
Then wish he could just disappear
For my sake.

"You ain't too heavy,"
I will interrupt, by way of pushing the number five
To accept another collect call
"You are my brother."

And for 15 minutes
We will remember ourselves as we dreamed.

And in those lives
One of us was always willing to lead,
And in those lives,
One of us was always willing to follow,

Because yesterday
I knew that I was my brothers' keeper

And today,
I know that nothing has changed.

WHEN THE REVOLUTION COMES

You say you want a revolution!
You say you want a revolution?
You say you want a revolution....
Well, you know
We all want to save the world,

But, but, but,
My Lexus just got recalled,

And, and, and,
Miss Cleo say, "My sign done gone inta retrograde."

So, so, so
I might just have to catch the highlights from home
When the revolution comes.

But when the revolution comes
Artificially impregnated,
Radiation induced,
Super germinated corn-fed babies
Will rise up and storm the halls of
Honors Science, English and Math.

They will refuse to go quietly or
Orderly back to their applied physics class
No longer willing to practice
The proper way to lift garbage cans.
They will demand to be served
What the good rich kids have been eating...

I think ya'll gone be surprised to know
What the masses have been teaching themselves,
When the revolution comes.

Cause when the revolution comes
Corner office pimps and penthouse hustlers
I mean, Wall Street brokers and
Corporate executive officers
Will be seen flinging themselves
From ledges and bridges and roofs.

In a final fit of cowardice
Aimed at saving them from the righteous rage
Of the poor whose backs their spiked heels climbed upon.

But much to their chagrin they will find
The "workers" have installed cages, nets and air bags
To ensure the continued safety of the power elite...
And having devised more effective ways
to dispose of this waste,
I'm pretty sure they won't be singing "Kumbaya"
When the revolution comes.

See, when the revolution comes
"Men who play God" will air on Dr. Phil
And y'all better not act surprised
When you see who is sitting in the hot seat
Next to Adolf, Saddam and O. Bin Laden

When they air a special segment titled
"We Be Hypocrites and Shit,"
You'll hear from the moral folks who demand

all babies should live
But ignore and refuse
To feed or nurture "the damn things" once they take a first
breath.

When the revolution comes
Somebody will scream
What the fuck do you mean
You may have "accidentally" overstated the imminent danger
inherent
In allowing oil rich politicians to misinform me?"

The GOP reiterate that
Lying about a blowjob is an
Affront to the American people,
And silently kneeling during the national anthem
Is an act of anti-patriotism,

But booing a black Commander in Chief,
Now that's an exercise in the expression of freedom.

Storming the Capitol
Is a demonstration of the people's will.

And ignoring the poor…
Well, that's just damn good for business.

But I bet a lot more people
Will be wishing they just took the blow job
When the revolution comes.

Cause when the revolution come poor whites

Will finally recognize their centuries long manipulation,
Strategically pitted against their most natural allies
Since before the opening volley of that uncivil war.

When the revolution comes
Reservations will rise up and open their borders
To the other Americans,
And together will outrageously demand
Payment on the promise signed in their blood.

Then, brown and black and tans and whites
Will blend into one mighty voice demanding
All our children raise heads higher,
Refusing to allow any child to avert their gaze,
Ensuring that generations understand
That today we are walking out of the shadows
So, they need not fear the darkness again.

Yeah, I think the whole world will be working overtime
When the revolution comes.

When the revolution comes
Jesus Christ God Almighty will rise again
And revoke his corporate sponsorship.

His first official miracle
Will be the rebuke of the pulpit thumping mega priest
who pimped his name for a
GOD *plus* **ME = SUV**
Bumper sticker.

Then he will be seen in all the wrong places,

And he will be seen with all the wrong people
Because we will be there for all the right reasons,
And a lot of people are gonna wish
They had read the whole damn book
When the revolution comes.

You Say you want a revolution!
You Say you want a revolution?
You Say you want a revolution....
Well, you know,
We all want to save the world.

But, but, but,
Homeland security didn't approve your shade of brown

And, and, and,
Your portfolio took a hit this quarter

So, so, so
You'll probably just download the speeches from you tube

Yeah, I 'm not sure you'll be ready to stand up
When the revolution comes.

PHONE MAN

She carefully scans the booth on their approach,
Notes the shattered privacy doors,
Then slowly enters,
Two children quietly trail her path.

Lifting the receiver, a handkerchief appears
Like magic in her left hand
To render this object safe for her young.

She digs through pockets.
They know she refuses to memorize the number.
Frustration begins restricting her smile as Junior
Begins to recite numbers like a mantra.
As she dials, her forced smile slowly fades.

With each undetected punch of buttons, she questions.
Why make all the effort reaching out to a man
That she should never have trusted?

But a glance left and right at her oldest two,
Four beautiful brown eyes is all the answer she ever needs.

"Yes operator."
Her voice toughens,
"This is a collect call...
You can say it is from his children."

Before the phone can connect
To the other end of their reality,

She passes the receiver to Theresa.

A long second of silence
Then the girl's spirit races into a fevered pitch.
Every laugh, cry, smile, and tear these two weeks
Resurface, dancing across young eyes.

Mother watches, as right beside her
A voice seven hundred miles away
Makes this child, temporarily, whole again.

The girl nods and mother sighs,
Knowing that the phone makes promises
That only the mother born of sacrifice will ever keep.

She motions. It's time for the boy.
But, she thinks, he is so different.

He speaks,
And she wonders,
"Does he believe the voice on the other side shares his blood?"

Brown eyes dart from glass, to wall, to mother, to ground.
And, she wonders,
"What must he think of the other boy?"

That boy who sleeps in his bed,
Goes to his school,
Dreams his perfect life beside the voice on the phone
For thirteen days, twenty-three hours, and fifty minutes.

But this one is so hard to read.

Only ten,
He has learned well to wear this armor of dark skin,
And wield this shield of early manhood
For maximum protection.

Soon she takes the phone,
Turns her back to them.
Her voice becomes a distant thunder,
Low and strong.

"I still have not received the support check
from two months ago...

Your daughter needs to get glasses . . .
The least you could do is
Put her back on your family insurance...

Don't forget your son has a birthday soon.

Well, maybe this year you can remember
and send him a card.

Right...
we're taking up your family time.
Yeah, two weeks."

Wearily she hangs the phone,
The children avert their gaze,
Try hard not to see the tears that swell to overflowing
And run down a quivering cheek.
In three seconds the tears are gone, but she is still there.
The calming force in their chaotic world.

Turning sharply into the wind,
She balances her soul.
One child secured in each hand,
She leads her oldest back into the concrete canyons
She carves with bare hands,
To protect them for the coming rains.

ON AND UP

When I was eight years old, I faltered and fell.
She picked me up then brushed me off,
And sent me onward and up.

When I was eleven, I faltered and failed.
She picked me up then brushed me off
And sent me onward and up.

At nineteen I faulted and failed
She helped me up, brushed me off
And sent me onward and up

For all of my life I never wanted to seem
Lost, useless, or without hope
In her eyes.

She tells me now
That for all of my life I have never seemed
Lost, useless, or without hope
In her eyes.

She asked me to speak the thunder.
She taught me to shout the lightning,
Then she demanded I consume the sun.

So, I did, and I do, and I will
Because she said I could.

She is inspiration,

The catcher of dreams,
My source of light.

But what she gave to me,
She offered to the world,
Refusing to wait
For others to make it right.

FOR THERESA

Only one had come before me,
Crossing the line
Barely a year ahead of the game.
This may have marked the first in a lifetime of relays.

We began racing
Through the foothills and ghettos of our youth
Facing mother against father,
Truth against lies.
Always we two jockeyed for position.

Like this we grew,
Sometimes in spite of each other.
In our moments of separation, it seems
We made our greatest leaps toward center.

We continued,
Not knowing that the way had been paved
For our sibling rivalry to blossom
Into respect and the love we seem
To draw from each other to survive.

Then once again you beat me
As the fruit of adulthood grew
And fell ripe from your strong rooted limbs.
You named this yam Imani -- Faith,
And the next to come was Tia.

Now our children fill the days with smiles

And memories of our own youth.

And as you and I complete our race
We can take time out to watch them grow,
Bearing witness as new contests begin.

MONDAY AT THE SOCIAL SECURITY OFFICE

Opening the doors
Blank faces greet,
Then turn,
Disinterested.

Take a number, fifty-nine.
Sit uncomfortable. Don't stare.

A neon board explains the procedure
A very alert elderly woman watches intently,
But the lights mean nothing to her

That man at the counter, number twenty-seven,
Is trying to explain how his wife died
Without having another breakdown.

Number thirty-eight, a mother
Rehearses her answers for a closed office audit.
Her child sits pensive, aware, and silent.

Number sixty-five opens a coke,
And everyone wonders why
They didn't think to bring one.

But no one speaks,
Just listening,
Trying not to hear the pain.

Number forty-four coughs,

Black-lung, I think.

Number eighty-six scans the room,
A blind gaze focused on whispered thoughts.

Soon people lose color,
Only numbers remain,
Marking us,
Refugees of this camp

"Number fifty-eight," a hollow voice finally shrieks,
And a young man rises.

"I was here before him!"
The old woman next to me screams, to herself.

I consider her for a moment
"Excuse me ma'am,"
I say, interrupting her silent rage.
"I think, maybe, you dropped your number,"
I point to a slip of paper at her feet.

She leans suspiciously toward the ticket,
Her eyes never quite leaving me.

"What number is this?"
She whispers to the man on her other side
"Fifty-nine," he says glancing at me.
"I guess that means you're next, ma'am."

See, the neon board is clear:
• If • You • Do • Not • Have • A • Number •

• You • Will • Not • See • A • Representative •

So,
Take a number, one hundred and five!
Sit uncomfortable,
Don't stare,
"Excuse me,"
 I say to Number sixty-five.
"Where is the Coke machine?"

FOR MORE THAN OURSELVES

There is a war raging in our front yard.
It consumes our youth, our race, and our soul,
Rending, without resistance, at the core of our humanity.
And no one wants to fight, because no one wants to sacrifice,
but

> Without sacrifice there will be no resistance,
> Without resistance there will be no hope,
> Without hope there will be no peace.

For more than ourselves we raise a fist,
Knowing that we are not the first.
We hope we will not be the last to volunteer.

There are black hearts festering in our back yard,
Threatening to annihilate an entire generation of our youth.
From the inside, blind oppression locked and cocked
Like an UZI pinned against their heads
And no one wants to witness, because no one wants to
sacrifice, but

> Without sacrifice there will be no understanding,
> Without understanding there will be no validation,
> Without validation there will be no justice.

For more than ourselves we raise our eyes
To view the world without the aid of color filters.
We refuse to avert our gaze,
Not because we like what we see,
But because we must witness the atrocity
And give testimony on behalf of the victims
If justice is to rise again.

There are voiceless children dying in our alley's,
Dreams crystallized like the crack inside their lungs.
They cannot scream in self-defense.
No one wants to hear their lifeless cries, because no one wants
to sacrifice, but
>Without sacrifice there will be no rehabilitation
>Without rehabilitation there will be no unity
>Without unity there will be no tomorrow.

For more than ourselves we raise our voices,
Stifle the urge to cringe in fear and seclusion.
We are the advocates of those who would be silenced.
Our time has come to speak.

For more than ourselves,
>We stand at the edge of oblivion, and peer into the darkness.

For more than ourselves,
>We raise a fist to beat back stark oppression.

For more than ourselves,
>We give the war cry that will herald a new
generation of hope.

ROOT LADY

"Our children are dying!" the voice thundered.
Spinning towards the boom brought me face to face with her,
The root lady.

A wild woman with lines in her face,
Each a story older than my father's father.
The wisdom in her left eye alone
Commanded I stand tall and take note of her prophetic verse.

She shook a solid left fist at me.
Furious bones wailed, demanded release,
But with much work before they would settle to the earth and
wait to be buried.

Casting her lot against the earthen wall
She spoke in the clik - clik tones of ancient tongues.
"You have choices to make," she said
In a language I never heard but the urgency was clear enough.

With that she reached for me,
Tore my beating heart from my chest.
"How many lives can one heart serve?" She questioned.
I searched my soul, sure that this was a trick.

"One I guess."

"And that is why you are destined to repeat the mistakes that
have brought you to me."
Tossing my heart, still beating, to the ground,

She began to walk away slowly.

"Leave It," she said
As I stooped to correct my anatomy.
"It will do you no good if you cannot hear it speak."

She commanded. I followed.

"You have evaded bullets, but they can still kill if you are not
prepared.
You have slipped the bonds, but they can still strangle if you
are not aware.
You have made life, but it will not survive if you are not willing
to sacrifice."

"You are a Black Man in America.
These trials have made you what you are
Just as they have unmade thousands before you.
Do not let their lessons go unlearned."

Now again she asked, "How many lives can one heart serve?"
As I kneeled to retrieve that part of me that had been
discarded,
I returned her question with a question,
"Old Lady," I returned,
"How many do you count among the oppressed and the
wronged and the damned?"

To my response
She smiled broadly,
Blew one last breath across me and began to fade from my
dreams.

COME WEDNESDAY

Come Wednesday
I will kiss my partner good morning,
I will turn on the hallway lights
Then, I will wake my kids for school.

Come Wednesday
I will return to my unfinished Tuesday work
on behalf of all children and families in America.

Come Wednesday
My America will not have fallen into chaos,
even if **my** candidate did not win the seats of power

Come Wednesday
I will accept the election of new leaders
As a statement from those who chose to be heard.
But I will not accept their election as a raging scream
Powerful enough to drown out the voices and rights of all the
"other" Americans

Because my America is greater than
The rhetoric of fear that has spewed
Uncorked from every orifice of this political machine.

And my American is stronger than
The identity politics that seek every nook and cranny
Of human difference, hoping to widen the gaps within U.S.

Come Wednesday
I will choose to walk another mile with people
Who do not look like me.

Come Wednesday
I will choose to discuss our future potential with people
Who do not talk like me

Come Wednesday
I will choose to offer an affirming hug or strong supporting
hand
To anyone who may have need of them,
Even if they had never imagined we could stand taller together

Come Wednesday
I will still be an American who grew up in the South

Come Wednesday
I will still be an American of African descent

Come Wednesday
I will still be a proud American who has:
Meditated with Buddha,
Fasted with Allah,
Lit candles with Yahweh, and
Prayed with God
And not one time felt
an imposter,
or betrayer,
or fool.

So,

Come Wednesday
I guess I will keep my own promise of
Making America Greater,
 again

Just like I have done at the break of every other new day
I have been blessed to meet.

Come Wednesday
I hope you will join me
On this long, worn road
Into tomorrow.

WE ARE

We are Bean Pies and Burritos,
Brats and Baklava,
Fry Bread, Bok Choy, and Biscuits.
We are Soul Food,
We are Soul Full,
We are So Full
of Life
of Hope
of Dreams,
That we span the continents
And time.

We are analysts and catalysts,
Trouble shooters and troublemakers,
Biking, walking, flying to the edge of our passions,
Then throwing ourselves into the mix.

We are teaching and learning,
Preaching and yearning.
We yearn to be heard
But not as a voice.
We are a movement in four parts.

We are film makers and risk takers,
Inspired by the best women produce,
Awed by the worst mankind has accomplished.

We are weavers,
But not just of fabric or tales or history.

We weave communities, spirits, and minds,
Designing the rich tapestry of our own future.

We are business as usual,
But there is nothing usual
About the business we have taken up.

We are dynamic in force,
Not able to stand suspended,
Wasting energy, wasting time, wasting life.

We are seven generations strong,
Three before us set the course,
Three behind will reap the victory.

And like the pyramids of the sun, we will rise to face the world.
Defying science, we confirm the indomitable spirit of our
humanity.

We are wisdom, glowing bright in young eyes,
Worn proud in experienced smiles.

We are They and Them
We are Y'all and Us

We are straight, and
We are gay, and
And we are questioning.

We are questioning,
Why do you want in our bedrooms?
Is it cause you want to join in?

Or are you just trying to close the closet door?

Cause this ain't Pandora's Box, baby,
But we are coming out.

"I'm coming out."

That's right, we are coming out and we want the world to know.

We want the world to know that
This bra doesn't fit, and we are not going to wear it.

We want the world to know that
Black will not sit in back.

We want the world to know that
Straight doesn't mean narrow,
Not in focus, not in love, not in our lives.

We are sons and daughters,
Mothers and fathers,
Some grand, some great, all young at heart.

We are survivors of urban sprawls
And dreamers of rural expanses.

We are American!
    By birth,
    By right,
    By choice!
So, we are the ones we've been waiting for.

We have been waiting for a sign.
We have been waiting for the keys.
We have been waiting for the truth.
Cause we can handle the truth,
And the truth will set us free,
Free to pursue justice
Because we will beat injustice down.

We are the American way,
At least the American dream.
Manifested or not, it has become our destiny.

We are human capital,
Waiting for our return on investments
    Of time,
    Of prayer,
    Of love.

So...
We are learning to trust, and
We are trying to build, and
We are willing to fail,
Refusing to sit passive,
Waiting for others to act.

We are the next generation,
Not to be confused with the first generation,
Not content to be the last iteration.
We are simply the next incarnation of the world we dream.

We are of ancient thoughts!
We are of universal truths!

We are of unwavering faith!
And,
We are just getting started!
And
We are just getting started!!
And
We

    Are

       Just

          Getting

             Started!!!

To live…
To love…
Together.
But now,
We are …

9/12

Today I wish you
strength in your weakest moment,
confidence in your times of doubt
hope in your darkest hour

Take a moment to remember
the distinct times in our national memory where we
stood up for,
stood behind,
stood beside,
each other
unflinching

the fact that we did not
look like,
think like,
act like,
pray like, or
love like each other
Almost confirmed in our hearts and minds
the greatness we could achieve as a united people.

Unfortunately,
those moments often come
when we are
in crisis,
filled with loss
succumbing to doubt.

But
each day we get to imagine
What if…
we give ourselves permission to always be that great

And
each day we get to ask
What kind…
of change could we bring to the world

then
each day we could stand and shout
why not…
Own our difference and acknowledge this amazing diversity
as the undeniable source of future greatness.

Looking back to yesterday
I inhale, deep
reflecting on those whose lives were lost
through selfless sacrifice
I exhale, long
Remembering the many more whose lives were taken
by selfish sacrifice

With the realization that we all still struggle
Each in our own way
to find hope
to keep faith
in our shared humanity.

Looking forward to tomorrow
I send up love and prayers

to all of those still in harm's way,

in a world where so many struggle daily for another moment
of safety,
of courage,
of hope,
of life.
I am reminded
That Hope does not come by chance,
But by choice.
So, today
I choose to act

ABOUT THE AUTHOR

Hasan Davis, J.D. began writing poetry at an early age with the encouragement of his mother, who he refers to as the international word wizard, Alice Lovelace, and his father, local Reggae Legend, Charles "Jikki" Riley.

Following them across the city of Atlanta, I witnessed the birth of spoken word from two pioneers of the art.
Initially, I think it was intended to occupy my time and energy, keep me out of trouble.

But there was no place that I would rather have been than in the front row mouthing along to their lyrical celebration of life, pain, and struggle like I was lip-syncing Stevie Wonder. This was how I learned to make sense of the chaos in the world I was navigating every day. Growing up experiencing ADHD and Dyslexia, I first created works with a natural cadence meant to be heard more than for reading.

Hasan's mentor and forensics coach, Harry Robie, encouraged him and helped him believe that he had a gift for telling full, well-rounded stories in just a few minutes.

Throughout college and law school this gift won me open mics, talent shows, poetry, and speech competitions to help pay the bills.

In time Hasan began to feel as if the issues and experiences that had sparked the anger and the creativity that fueled his pen had passed. He put away his words and began new work through living history interpretation and advocacy work focused on the pressing issues facing disconnected and disenfranchised communities. Recently, Hasan pulled his old poetry notebooks out and to his disappointment realized the experience of his early writing was as relevant to the issues of justice, access, and opportunity in 2021 as they were in 1990.

So, here we are.

Hasan Davis is a Hope Dealer.

Growing up in the south in the 1970s and '80s wasn't easy. between the overt racism and schools that did not seem interested or prepared to support me I the way I needed to find success navigating my learning challenges. That kind of frustration easily turns to anger and just feeds itself. When I was eleven, I was arrested and adjudicated delinquent by the state of Georgia. I was on probation for the rest of my childhood. After my 7th-grade school year, my mother enrolled me in an alternative school. A last-ditch effort to give me the kind of learning environment I could thrive in. Though I found some success and developed confidence in my ability to overcome obstacles, I was expelled my senior year.

After years of navigating the streets, I knew what others saw when they looked at me, a menace, a monster, but I didn't care. I had learned to wear my armor of rage and anger as a warning to the world, don't mess with me or mine. I never forgot the words my mother spoke to me on that long ride home from the police station all those years ago. When looked at me with tears rolling down her face and said, "If you could see what I see, every time I look at you, then you would know how great you already were." I was still looking for that guy and wanted more than ever to be the man my momma imagined and spoke into the world that night.

Hasan's persistence paid off as he earned his GED. Then decided that college would be his next big step.

This was a crossroads for me. I was still struggling, but I really wanted to make it. And for the first time I think I finally understood that the only person who could stop me from succeeding was me.

Today, Hasan has a bachelor's degree and a Juris Doctorate. He has served as Director of youth violence Prevention for the city of Lexington Kentucky and Commissioner of Juvenile Justice for the Commonwealth of Kentucky.

Hasan is transforming systems to ensure that all students are safe, supported, and on a clear path to success. As Commissioner of Juvenile Justice for the Commonwealth of Kentucky, Hasan led a comprehensive juvenile justice reform effort that resulted in the passage of legislation that dramatically transformed the work of child-serving systems across the Commonwealth. As a member of the Federal Advisory Committee on Juvenile Justice, Hasan provided guidance to Congress and the executive branch around the importance of racial equity in the operationalization of the Juvenile Justice and Delinquency Prevention Act. Hasan is an Education Trust Family Fellow, a Rockefeller Foundation next generation leadership Fellow, an Annie E. Casey children and family Fellow, and a Council of State Governments Henry Toll Fellow.

Hasan is committed to empowering young people and adults by assisting them in finding their voice, personal power, sense of self-respect, and dignity. He uses his passion for theater and the arts to ensure educators and leaders understand issues of equity and their role in ensuring all young people are engaged, encouraged, and empowered. He is internationally recognized as a speaker, educator, and advocate for youth.

Each of us has a right to become the hero of our own story.
Some of us just need more help finding the right cape ... and comfy boots!

an imprint of Martin Sisters Publishing Company, Inc.

Made in the USA
Middletown, DE
07 April 2024

52551465R00096